CHOCOLATE BOX

Cakes & Biscuits

Joanna Farrow

HARLAXTON
PUBLISHING

Harlaxton Publishing Limited   2 Avenue Road
Grantham
Lincolnshire
NG31 6TA United Kingdom
A Member of the Weldon International Group of Companies

First published 1994
© 1994 Copyright: Harlaxton Publishing Limited
© 1994 Copyright design: Harlaxton Publishing Limited

Publisher: Robin Burgess
Publishing Manager & Design: Rachel Rush
Editor: Alison Leach
Illustrator: Lyne Breeze, Linden Artists
Photographer: James Duncan
Home Economist: Sue Maggs
Recipes: Joanna Farrow
Cover: Sue Maggs
Stylist: Madelaine Brehaut
Typesetter: John Macauley, Seller's
Colour separation: GA Graphics
Printer: Mandarin, Hong Kong

British Library Cataloguing-in-Publication data
Title: Chocolate Box: Cakes and Biscuits
ISBN: 1-85837-144-9

Contents

Dark, delicious and irresistibly indulgent, chocolate is greeted with more enthusiasm than any other food. Its inimitable texture, which melts, blends, models and moulds, gives it a unique versatility, whether you are serving chocolate chip cookies or an elaborate gâteau.

Supermarkets and confectioners stock a wide range of different chocolates, so it is worth knowing a little about the processing of chocolate before making your choice.

Chocolate is taken from the cacao pod, harvested from the cacao tree which thrives mainly in Africa, Brazil and Malaysia. After harvesting, the pods are split to reveal cocoa beans. These are sun-fermented for several days to develop their 'chocolatey' flavour. After shelling and roasting, the beans are pressed to produce 'cocoa solids'. The chocolate we buy contains varying quantities of these solids, usually with added sugar and milk. Generally, the higher the percentage of cocoa solids contained in chocolate, the better the flavour and, hence, suitability for special cakes and desserts.

Opposite: Types of chocolate.

Types of Chocolate

Bitter (Semisweet) Chocolate

This is the richest type of chocolate you can buy, containing about 70% solids. It is generally preferred by chocolate 'connoisseurs' who find other types of chocolate too sweet. Bitter chocolate can be used instead of plain (dark) in cooking when you want a really rich flavour.

Plain (Dark) Chocolate

This contains varying amounts of sugar and cocoa solids (anywhere between about 30% and 60%). In the supermarkets it is either stocked on the confectionery counter, or with other types of cooking chocolate.

Milk Chocolate

This contains less cocoa solids (usually around 20%) and has a lot of sugar and milk added. Not surprisingly, when melted and blended with other ingredients, the chocolate flavour and colour become rather 'diluted'. Like plain (dark) chocolate, it is either stocked on the confectionery counter, where you might find one with a higher quantity of cocoa solids, or with other types of cooking chocolate.

White Chocolate

This contains cocoa butter (extracted during processing) rather than cocoa solids. Large quantities of sugar and milk are added to produce its sweet, creamy flavour. White chocolate will not set as solidly as plain and has a greater tendency to burn.

Chocolate-Flavour Cake Covering

This is the cheapest form of chocolate and has the least 'chocolatey' flavour. It is made from sugar, vegetable oil, cocoa and flavouring and has a fatty, bland flavour. Although inferior in quality, a little added to plain (dark) or milk chocolate when melting makes it more stable and easier to shape into curls and other decorations.

Cocoa Powder

This is made when much of the naturally occurring cocoa butter is removed from the chocolate after roasting. It is usually used to replace some of the flour in chocolate cakes. Drinking chocolate is a mixture of cocoa, sugar and, sometimes, dried milk powder. It is unsuitable for cooking but can be used to dust over cakes and desserts.

Melting Chocolate

There are two easy ways to melt chocolate: in a bowl over hot water or in a microwave.

Saucepan Method

Break the chocolate into even-sized pieces and place in a heatproof bowl. Rest the bowl over a pan of gently simmering water and leave until melted. The bowl should fit snugly into the pan but must not touch the water level or the chocolate will become overheated.

Once the bowl is removed, make sure no condensation drips into the chocolate or it will 'seize' into a solid mass. Chocolate should only be melted directly in a pan when other liquids are added.

Microwave Method

Break the chocolate into even-sized pieces and place in a microwave-proof bowl. Microwave on Medium setting allowing 2 minutes for 60g/2 oz/2 squares chocolate and 3 minutes for 225g/8 oz/8 squares chocolate. When butter or syrup is melted with the chocolate, it will take less time. Leave to stand briefly after melting, then stir gently.

Decorative Ideas

A scattering of grated chocolate or chocolate curls can add the finishing touch to any chocolate cake or gâteau. Once made, the curls will keep in a cool, dry place for a couple of weeks.

Simple Chocolate Curls

Use a large bar of plain (dark), milk or white chocolate at room temperature, and pare with a swivel-handled potato peeler. If the chocolate is too cold, it will break into brittle splinters and can be microwaved very briefly before trying again.

Chocolate Caraque

Melt about 175g/6 oz/6 squares plain, milk or white chocolate and spread thinly on a marble slab, smooth work surface (counter) or large baking sheet. Leave until set but not brittle. Draw a knife, held at an angle of 45°, across the chocolate to remove small curls. Alternatively, push a clean wallpaper scraper across the chocolate to remove larger curls. If the chocolate breaks into brittle pieces, it is probably too cold and should be left at room temperature before trying again.

Modelling Chocolate

This is a pliable paste which can be modelled into decorative shapes for decorating cakes and gâteaux, see the Easter Celebration Gâteau (p.64). Fun to use, it can also be made into novelty decorations such as teddy bears and flowers. It will keep in the refrigerator for up to 2 weeks.

Melt 125g/4 oz/4 squares plain (dark), milk or white chocolate. Beat in 2 tablespoons liquid glucose or golden (light corn) syrup until a paste is formed which comes away from the sides of the bowl. Place in a thick plastic bag and leave until firm and pliable. Shape small pieces in the palms of your hands or roll thinly on a work surface (counter) lightly dusted with icing (confectioners') sugar.

Gooey, mouthwatering chocolate cakes are, for many of us, what cooking with chocolate is all about. A generous slice of Rich Chocolate Fudge Cake (p.17), dripping with thick cream is the ultimate, thoroughly wicked treat. Just as exciting is the Chocolate-cased Fruit Gâteau (p.20), oozing chocolate cream, or a freshly baked Chocolate Mousse Cake (p.15), the most moist cake imaginable – a must for those who have not tasted one before.

Teabreads provide a quick and easy variation on the cake theme. Simple to prepare, their irresistible aroma when cooling makes them impossible to resist, rather like freshly baked bread.

Previous page: Chocolate Cake with Brandied Figs and Swiss Roll with Chocolate Cream.

Chocolate Cake with Brandied Figs

Serves 12	225g/8 oz/1 cup soft margarine
	225g/8 oz/1 cup caster (superfine) sugar
	4 eggs
	200g/7 oz/1¾ cups self-raising flour
	30g/1 oz/¼ cup cocoa powder
	2 teaspoons baking powder
	1 tablespoon milk

Filling:	125g/4 oz/1 cup dried figs
	½ teaspoon cornflour (cornstarch)
	3 tablespoons brandy
	150ml/¼ pint/⅔ cup Greek yoghurt

| Icing: | 200g/7 oz/7 squares plain (dark) chocolate |
| | 300ml/½ pint/1¼ cups double (heavy) cream |

| To Decorate: | Chocolate caraque (p.7) |
| | Icing (confectioners') sugar for dusting |

Grease and base-line two 20cm/8 inch sandwich tins (layer pans). Place the margarine, sugar and eggs in a bowl. Sift the flour, cocoa powder and baking powder into the bowl and beat with an electric whisk until creamy and paler in colour. Beat in the milk.

Divide the mixture between the prepared tins and level the surfaces. Bake in a preheated oven at 170°C/325°F/gas 3 for 25–30 minutes until well risen and just firm to the touch. Transfer to a wire rack to cool.

To make the filling, chop the figs and place in a saucepan with 150ml/¼pint/⅔ cup water. Bring to the boil, reduce the heat and simmer gently for 5 minutes. Blend the cornflour with a little water and add to the pan. Cook, stirring continuously, until thickened. Remove from the heat and stir in the brandy. Leave to cool.

Place one cake on a serving plate and spread with the yoghurt. Spoon over the fig mixture and cover with second cake. To make the icing, break the chocolate into pieces. Heat the cream in a saucepan, then stir in the chocolate until it has melted. Leave to cool slightly, then beat the icing and swirl over top and sides of the cake.

Scatter the chocolate caraque over the cake and serve dusted with icing sugar.

Variation
Substitute dried prunes, apricots or dates for the figs.

Swiss Roll with Chocolate Cream

Serves 8

3 eggs
90g/3 oz/ ⅓ cup caster (superfine) sugar
½ teaspoon ground cinnamon
75g/2½ oz/generous ½ cup plain (all-purpose) flour
2 tablespoons cocoa powder

Filling:

150ml/¼ pint/⅔ cup double (heavy) cream
2 teaspoons icing (confectioners') sugar
90g/3 oz/¾ cup plain (dark) or milk chocolate chips
Icing (confectioners') sugar for dusting

Grease and line a 33x23cm/13x9 inch Swiss (jelly) roll tin (pan) with greased non-stick baking parchment.

Place the eggs, sugar and cinnamon in a heatproof bowl over a saucepan of simmering water. Beat with an electric whisk until the mixture leaves a trail when the whisk is lifted from the bowl. Remove from the heat and continue whisking until cooled. Sift together the flour and cocoa powder, and fold into the mixture carefully, using a large metal spoon.

Spoon into the prepared tin and ease the mixture gently into the corners. Bake in a preheated oven at 200°C/400°F/ gas 6 for about 15 minutes until just firm to the touch. Place a sheet of greaseproof paper on a work surface (counter) and sprinkle with caster sugar. Invert the cake on the paper and peel away the lining paper. Starting from a short side, roll up the cake with the paper and leave to cool.

To make the filling, whip the cream with the icing sugar until it is just peaking. Stir in the chocolate chips. Unroll the cake carefully and spread with the cream mixture. Roll up again and transfer to a serving plate. Serve dusted with icing sugar.

Chocolate Ripple Teabread

Serves 12   200g/7 oz/17 squares plain (dark) chocolate
plus 60g/2 oz/2 squares plain (dark) or milk chocolate to decorate
200g/7 oz/scant 1 cup unsalted butter or margarine
175g/6 oz/¾ cup caster (superfine) sugar
3 eggs
200g/7 oz/1¾ cups self-raising flour
½ teaspoon baking powder
2 teaspoons milk

Lightly grease the base and long sides of a 900g/2 lb loaf tin (pan). Break the plain chocolate into pieces and melt in a heatproof bowl with 30g/1oz/2 tablespoons of the butter or margarine over a saucepan of simmering water.

Place the remaining butter or margarine in a bowl with the sugar, eggs, flour and baking powder. Beat until light and fluffy; then beat in the milk.

Spoon a quarter of the cake mixture into the prepared tin and level the surface. Spread with a third of the chocolate mixture. Spread with another quarter of the cake mixture and another third of the chocolate. Repeat layering, finishing with a layer of the cake mixture.

Chop the chocolate into small pieces and scatter down the centre of the mixture. Bake in a preheated oven at 180°C/350°F/gas 4 for about 1 hour until risen and a skewer inserted into the centre comes out clean. Leave in the tin for 10 minutes before transferring to a wire rack to cool completely.

Right: Left to right, Chocolate Ripple Teabread and Spicy Fruit Teabread.

Spicy Fruit Teabread

Serves 12-14

300g/10 oz/2 cups mixed dried fruit
175g/6 oz/1 cup light muscovado sugar
300ml/½ pint/1¼ cups cold tea
225g/8 oz/2 cups self-raising flour
30g/1oz/¼ cup cocoa powder
1 teaspoon ground mixed (apple pie) spice
½ teaspoon bicarbonate of soda (baking soda)
1 egg
45g/1½ oz/3 tablespoons stem (candied) ginger, finely chopped
2 tablespoons sunflower seeds

Grease and line the base and long sides of a 900g/2 lb loaf tin. Place the mixed dried fruit in a saucepan with the sugar and tea, and bring to the boil. Remove from the heat and leave to cool completely.

Sift the flour, cocoa powder, mixed spice and bicarbonate of soda into a bowl. Add the egg, dried fruit mixture and ginger, and beat until the ingredients are evenly combined.

Turn into the prepared tin and level the surface. Sprinkle with the sunflower seeds and bake in a preheated oven at 180°C/350°F/gas 4 for 1¼–1½ hours until a skewer inserted into the centre comes out clean. Leave to cool in the tin for 10 minutes before transferring to a wire rack to cool completely.

Chocolate Spiced Parkin

Serves 16

45g/1½ oz/3 tablespoons stem ginger
225g/8 oz/⅔ cup black treacle (molasses)
225g/8 oz/⅔ cup golden (light corn) syrup
125g/4 oz/½ cup unsalted butter or margarine
½ teaspoon bicarbonate of soda (baking soda)
300ml/½ pint/1¼ cups milk
1 egg
350g/12 oz/3 cups plain (all-purpose) flour
125g/4 oz/1 cup cocoa powder
2 teaspoons ground ginger
350g/12 oz/scant 2½ cups medium oatmeal
60g/2 oz/¼ cup caster (superfine) sugar
Extra oatmeal for dusting

Grease and line a 23cm/9 inch square cake tin (pan). Slice the ginger as thinly as possible.

Place the treacle, syrup and butter or margarine in a saucepan and heat gently until the fat has melted. Mix together the bicarbonate of soda, milk and egg. Sift the flour and cocoa powder into a bowl. Stir in the oatmeal, sugar and two-thirds of the sliced ginger. Add the treacle mixture and stir until the ingredients are evenly combined. Spoon into the prepared tin and scatter with the reserved stem ginger. Bake in a preheated oven at 180°C/350°F/ gas 4 for about 45 minutes until just firm to touch. Dust with extra oatmeal and leave to cool in the tin.

Cook's Tip
Parkin is best eaten 2–3 days after cooking. When cooled, transfer the cake to an airtight tin.
Right: Chocolate Spiced Parkin.

Chocolate Mousse Cake

Serves 6-8

225g/8 oz/8 squares plain (dark) chocolate
125g/4 oz/½ cup unsalted butter
2 tablespoons Cointreau or orange-flavoured liqueur
Grated rind of 1 lemon
5 eggs, separated
125g/4 oz/½ cup caster (superfine) sugar
Icing (confectioners') sugar for dusting

Grease and line a 23cm/9 inch spring-release (spring form) or loose-based round cake tin (pan). Break the chocolate into pieces and place in a heatproof bowl with the butter. Rest over a pan of simmering water and leave until melted. Remove from the heat and stir in the liqueur and lemon rind.

Beat the egg yolks in a bowl with 60g/2 oz/¼ cup of the sugar until pale and creamy. Stir in the melted chocolate mixture.

Whisk the egg whites in a separate bowl until stiff. Whisk in the remaining sugar gradually. Using a large metal spoon, fold a quarter of the whites into the chocolate mixture. Fold in the remainder carefully. Spoon into the prepared tin and bake in a preheated oven at 170°C/ 325°F/gas 3 for about 30 minutes until well risen and the centre feels very spongy when pressed gently. Leave to cool in the tin before transferring to a serving plate. Serve dusted with icing sugar.

Cook's Tip

Because of its high egg content, this cake rises like a soufflé during cooking and then deflates gradually when removed from the oven. This produces a delicious cracked crust.

Chocolate Nut Genoise with Orange Frosting

Serves 10

60g/2 oz/½ cup brazil nuts
30g/1 oz/2 tablespoons unsalted butter
4 eggs
125g/4 oz/½ cup caster (superfine) sugar
90g/3 oz/¾ cup plain (all-purpose) flour
30g/1 oz/¼ cup cocoa powder
Grated chocolate to decorate

Frosting:

350g/12 oz/1½ cups full-fat soft cheese
2 tablespoons icing (confectioners') sugar
Grated rind of 1 orange
4-5 teaspoons orange juice

Grease and base line three 18cm/7 inch round sandwich tins (layer pans). Toast the nuts lightly and chop them. Melt the butter.

Place the eggs and sugar in a heatproof bowl over a saucepan of simmering water and whisk until the mixture leaves a trail when the whisk is lifted from the bowl. Remove from the heat and whisk until the mixture has cooled.

Sift the flour and cocoa powder together. Fold half into the egg mixture, then add the butter and nuts and fold in with the remaining flour. Divide the mixture between the prepared tins and bake in a preheated oven at 190°C/375°F/gas 5 for 20–25 minutes until risen and just beginning to shrink from the sides of the tin. Transfer to a wire rack to cool.

To make the frosting, beat the soft cheese in a bowl with the icing sugar and orange rind. Add enough orange juice to give a softly peaking consistency.

Place one cake on a serving plate and spread with a third of the frosting. Cover with another cake and spread with another third of the frosting. Finally, add the remaining cake and spread with the remaining frosting. Scatter with grated chocolate and keep in a cool place until ready to serve.

Chocolate Sandwich Cake

Serves 10-12

Cake

125g/4 oz/4 squares milk chocolate
225g/8 oz/1 cup soft margarine
225g/8 oz/1 cup caster (superfine) sugar
4 eggs
200g/7 oz/1¾ cups self-raising flour
30g/1 oz/¼ cup cocoa powder
2 teaspoons baking powder
1 tablespoon milk

To Decorate:

150ml/¼ pint/⅔ cup double (heavy) cream
2 teaspoons icing (confectioners') sugar
Extra icing (confectioners') sugar for dusting

Grease and base line two 20cm/8 inch sandwich tins (layer pans). Chop the chocolate roughly.

Place the margarine, sugar and eggs in a bowl. Sift the flour, cocoa powder and baking powder into the bowl, and beat with an electric whisk until creamy and paler in colour. Beat in the milk and chopped chocolate.

Divide the mixture between the prepared tins and level the surfaces. Bake in a preheated oven at 170°C/325°F/gas 3 for 25–30 minutes until well risen and just firm to touch. Transfer to a wire rack to cool.

To decorate the cake, whip the cream lightly with the

icing sugar and use to sandwich the cakes together. Serve generously dusted with icing sugar.

Variation

Mascarpone, a very mild, creamy low-fat cheese can be substituted for the cream in the filling. If liked, stir in some chopped walnuts or hazelnuts.

Rich Chocolate Fudge Cake

Serves 16	225g/8 oz/1 cup soft margarine
	350g/12 oz/2 cups light muscovado sugar
	4 eggs
	350g/12 oz/2 cups plain (all-purpose) flour
	1 tablespoon baking powder
	4 tablespoons golden (light corn) syrup
	125g/4 oz/1 cup cocoa powder
	150ml/¼ pint/⅔ cup soured cream
	150ml/¼ pint/⅔ cup double (heavy) cream
	1 tablespoon icing (confectioners') sugar
Icing:	275g/10 oz/10 squares plain (dark) chocolate
	60g/2 oz/¼ cup unsalted butter
	4 tablespoons milk
	225g/8 oz/1⅓ cups icing (confectioners') sugar
To Decorate:	Chocolate caraque (p.7)
	Icing (confectioners') sugar for dusting

Grease and line a 20cm/8 inch round cake tin (pan). Beat the margarine and sugar together until light and fluffy. Beat the eggs and beat into the creamed mixture gradually, adding a little of the flour to prevent the mixture from curdling. Sift the flour and baking powder into a separate bowl.

Mix together the syrup, cocoa powder and 175ml/6 floz/¾ cup warm water. Stir into the creamed mixture.

Fold half the sifted flour into the mixture; then fold in the soured cream and remaining flour. Spoon into the prepared tin and level the surface. Bake in a preheated oven at 150°C/300°F/gas 2 for about 1¼–1½ hours until well risen and a skewer inserted into the centre, comes out clean. Leave in the tin for 10 minutes before transferring to a wire rack to cool completely.

Whip the cream with the icing sugar. Split the cake in half and sandwich together with the cream. Place on a serving plate.

To make the icing, break the chocolate into pieces and place in a saucepan with the butter and milk. Heat gently until the chocolate has melted, stirring continuously. Beat in the icing sugar.

Let the icing cool slightly before swirling it over the top and sides of the cake. Scatter the top of the cake with chocolate caraque and serve dusted with icing sugar.

Cook's Tip

The chocolate caraque is not essential but it does make the cake look even more irresistible. Coarsely grated chocolate can be used as an easier alternative.

Next page: Left to right, Chocolate Nut Genoise with Orange Frosting and Chocolate Sandwich Cake.

Chocolate-cased Fruit Gâteau

Serves 10-12

4 eggs
125g/4 oz/⅔ cup light muscovado sugar
125g/4 oz/1 cup plain (all-purpose) flour
60g/2 oz/2 squares white chocolate, finely grated
175g/6 oz /6 squares plain (dark) chocolate

Filling:
450g/1 lb mixed soft fruit, such as strawberries,
raspberries, cherries, redcurrants and blackcurrants
2 tablespoons caster (superfine) sugar
4 tablespoons Kirsch
450ml/¾ pint/2 cups double (heavy) cream

Grease and line an 18cm/7 inch round cake tin (pan). Place the eggs and sugar in a heatproof bowl over a saucepan of simmering water and whisk until the mixture leaves a trail when the whisk is lifted from the bowl. Remove from the heat and whisk the mixture until it has cooled. Sift the flour over the mixture. Add the grated chocolate and fold in using a large metal spoon. Spoon into the prepared tin and bake in a preheated oven at 180°C/ 350°F/gas 4 for about 30 minutes until just firm to the touch. Transfer to a wire rack to cool.

To make the filling, mix the soft fruit in a bowl and add the sugar and Kirsch. Toss very gently. Whip the cream. Split the cake horizontally and place one half on a serving plate. Spread with a little of the cream and cover with half the fruit, reserving any excess juices that are left in the fruit bowl. Cover with the second half of the cake. Stir any juices into the remaining cream and swirl it over the top and sides of the cake.

Break the plain chocolate into pieces and melt in a

heatproof bowl over a saucepan of simmering water. Measure the circumference of the cake, using a piece of string. Cut a piece of greaseproof paper (baking parchment), 2.5cm/1 inch longer than the circumference and 2.5cm/1 inch deeper than the cake. Spread the melted chocolate over the paper, taking it to within 1cm/½ inch of the ends and in a wavy line about 1cm/½ inch from one long side. Spread chocolate almost to the edge of the remaining long side. Leave the chocolate until it is no longer runny, then carefully position it around the cake with the long straight edge around the base of the cake and the ends just touching down the side. Chill until the chocolate has set and then peel away the paper carefully. Just before serving, scatter the top of the cake with the reserved soft fruit.

Cook's Tip

The chocolate collar is surprisingly easy to position as long as you do so when the chocolate is no longer runny, but not yet beginning to set. If necessary, get someone to help to support the collar while you wrap it around the cake.

Left: Chocolate-cased Fruit Gâteau

Devils Food Cake with American Frosting

Serves 10-12 125g/4 oz/4 squares plain (dark) chocolate
250ml/8 fl oz/1 cup milk
225g/8 oz/2 cups plain (all-purpose) flour
½ teaspoon bicarbonate of soda (baking soda)
2 teaspoons baking powder
2 tablespoons cocoa powder
150g/5 oz/⅔ cup soft margarine
275g/10 oz/1¾ cups light muscovado sugar
3 eggs

Filling: 150ml/¼ pint/⅔ cup double (heavy) cream
3 tablespoons dark muscovado sugar

Frosting: 1 egg white
175g/6 oz/¾ cup caster (superfine) sugar
Pinch of cream of tartar

Grease and line the base and sides of an 18cm/7inch round cake tin (pan). Break the chocolate into pieces and place in a saucepan with the milk. Heat gently, stirring continuously until it has melted. Leave to cool.

Sift together the flour, bicarbonate of soda, baking powder and cocoa powder. Beat the margarine and sugar together until light and fluffy. Beat in the eggs gradually, adding a little of the flour to prevent the mixture from curdling. Fold in half the flour mixture, then the chocolate mixture. Fold in the remaining flour.

Spoon the mixture into the tin and bake in a preheated oven at 180°C/350°F/gas 4 for about 45 minutes until risen and a skewer inserted into the centre, comes out clean. Leave to cool in the tin.

To make the filling, whip the cream lightly. Cut the cake horizontally into three layers. Place one layer on a serving plate and spread with half the cream. Sprinkle with half the sugar. Cover with a second layer and cover with remaining cream and sugar. Cover with the remaining layer.

To make the frosting, place all the ingredients in a heatproof bowl with 2 tablespoons hot water. Rest over a saucepan of simmering water and beat with an electric whisk until the frosting stands in soft peaks. Spread the frosting immediately over the top and sides of the cake.

White Chocolate and Banana Teabread

Serves 12 150g/5 oz/5 squares white chocolate,
plus 45g/1½ oz/1½ squares white chocolate to decorate
3 small bananas
250g/9 oz/2¼ cups self-raising flour
1 teaspoon baking powder
135g/4½ oz/generous ½ cup unsalted butter or margarine
135g/4½ oz/generous ½ cup caster (superfine) sugar
Grated rind of 1 lemon
3 eggs

Grease and line the base and long sides of a 900g/2 lb loaf tin (pan). Chop the chocolate into small pieces. Peel and mash the bananas.

Sift the flour and baking powder into a bowl. Cut the butter or margarine into small pieces and rub into the flour with your fingertips. Add the sugar, lemon rind, eggs, banana and chocolate, and beat until the ingredients are evenly combined.

Spoon into the prepared tin and level the surface. Bake in a preheated oven at 180°C/350°F/gas 4 for about 50–60 minutes until well risen and a skewer inserted into the centre comes out clean. Leave in the tin for 10 minutes before transferring to a wire rack to cool completely.

To decorate the teabread, break the chocolate into pieces and melt in a heatproof bowl over a saucepan of simmering water. Using a teaspoon, drizzle the melted chocolate over the teabread and swirl lightly with the tip of a cocktail stick (toothpick). Leave to set.

Variation

Substitute plain (dark) or milk chocolate for the white and replace 30g/1 oz/¼ cup of the self-raising flour with cocoa powder. Add a little ground mixed (apple pie) spice if liked.

Chocolate Biscuit Pyramid

Serves 10-12

275g/10 oz digestive (graham crackers) or shortbread biscuits (cookies)
500g/18 oz/18 squares plain (dark) chocolate
350ml/12 fl oz/1½ cups evaporated milk
175g/6 oz/1½ cups mixed nuts, such as almonds, hazelnuts, peanuts and walnuts, roughly chopped
125g/4 oz/⅔ cup raisins
60g/2 oz/2 squares plain (dark) or white chocolate to decorate

Line the base and three sides of a 20cm/8 inch square cake tin (pan) with cling film (plastic wrap). Chop the biscuits into chunks.

Break the chocolate into pieces and place in a saucepan with the evaporated milk. Heat gently, stirring continuously until the chocolate has melted. Remove from the heat and transfer to a bowl. Leave to cool.

Stir the nuts into the chocolate mixture with the raisins and biscuits. Prop the prepared tin on a carton so that the base of the tin is tilted to an angle of 45° and the unlined side of the tin is uppermost. Spoon the cake mixture into the tin and level the surface. Leave to set.

Remove the cake carefully from the tin and peel away the cling film. Place on a serving plate. To decorate the cake, break the chocolate into pieces and melt in a heatproof bowl over a saucepan of simmering water. Place in a piping bag fitted with a writing tube (tip) and use to pipe decorative lines over the cake.

Keep in a cool place until ready to serve.

Cook's Tip

When the cake has hardened sufficiently, the tin can be transferred to the refrigerator to speed up setting. Remove from the refrigerator for about 30 minutes before serving to make slicing easier.

Crumbly biscuits and cookies, lavishly spread or speckled with melting chunks of chocolate, are fun to make and irresistibly 'moreish' to eat. This chapter includes a variety of shapes, sizes and textures, from huge American-style cookies to delicate wafer tuiles that make the perfect accompaniment to coffee, or to provide texture with a creamy chocolate pudding.

Home-made biscuits do not generally have the keeping qualities of bought biscuits, so avoid making up too many in one go. If a recipe makes more than required, refrigerate half the uncooked mixture and make up a fresh batch a day or so later. This applies in particular to gingerbread biscuits, macaroons and those made with porridge oats.

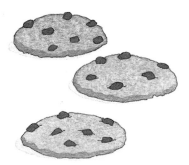

Previous page: Left to right, Double Chocolate Creams, White Chocolate Fingers and Cocoa Spice Biscuits.

White Chocolate Fingers

Makes about 12   60g/2 oz/½ cup flaked (slivered) almonds
60g/2 oz/2 squares white chocolate
60g/2 oz/¼ cup unsalted butter or margarine, softened
45g/1½ oz/3 tablespoons caster (superfine) sugar
Grated rind of 1 lemon
60g/2 oz/½ cup plain (all-purpose) flour
30g/1 oz/¼ cup ground almonds
Icing (confectioners') sugar for dusting

Grease a large baking sheet lightly. Break the flaked almonds roughly into smaller pieces. Chop the chocolate into small pieces.

Cream the butter or margarine and sugar together until light and fluffy. Stir in the lemon rind, flour, ground almonds and chopped chocolate to make a firm paste. Knead the mixture lightly, then roll out a quarter on a lightly floured work surface (counter) to a sausage, about 1cm/½ inch in diameter. Cut into 5cm/2 inch lengths. Roll in the flaked almonds until lightly coated; then transfer to the prepared baking sheet. Repeat with the remaining mixture.

Bake the biscuits in a preheated oven at 170°C/325°F/ gas 3 for about 8 minutes until turning golden. Leave on the baking sheet for 3 minutes before transferring to a wire rack to cool completely. Dust generously with icing sugar.

Variation
Use chopped plain (dark), milk or orange flavoured chocolate instead of the white. For a darker colouring replace 2 tablespoons of the flour with cocoa powder and dust with cocoa powder after baking

Cocoa Spice Biscuits

Makes 24

125g/4 oz/½ cup unsalted butter
or margarine, softened
125g/4 oz/⅔ cup light muscovado sugar
1 egg yolk
200g/7 oz/1¾ cups plain (all-purpose) flour
30g/1 oz/¼ cup cocoa powder
1 teaspoon ground mixed (apple pie) spice
60g/2 oz/⅓ cup sultanas
30g/1 oz/3 tablespoons currants
Milk to mix
Caster (superfine) sugar to sprinkle

Grease two baking sheets lightly. Cream together the butter or margarine and sugar until light and fluffy. Stir in the egg yolk. Sift the flour, cocoa powder and mixed spice into the bowl. Add the sultanas and currants, and mix to a firm dough, adding a little milk if the mixture is dry. Knead the dough lightly and roll out on a floured work surface (counter). Cut out 5cm/2 inch rounds, using a biscuit (cookie) cutter. Transfer the biscuits to the prepared baking sheets and sprinkle with caster sugar. Bake in a preheated oven at 170°C/350°F/gas 3 for 15–20 minutes until slightly darker. Leave on the baking sheets for 3 minutes before transferring to a wire rack to cool completely.

Double Chocolate Creams

Makes 15

160g/5½ oz/scant 1½ cups plain (all-purpose) flour
2 tablespoons cocoa powder
125g/4 oz/½ cup unsalted butter
60g/2 oz/¼ cup caster (superfine) sugar

To Finish:

60g/2 oz/2 squares white chocolate
Cocoa powder for dusting

Grease a large baking sheet lightly. Sift the flour and cocoa powder into a bowl. Cut the butter into small pieces and rub into the flour with your fingertips. Stir in the sugar and knead until the mixture makes a firm dough. (Alternatively, mix the ingredients to a dough in a food processor.)

Roll out the dough on a lightly floured work surface (counter) to a 27x19cm/10½x7½ inch rectangle. Transfer to the baking sheet and mark a 25x18cm/10x7 inch rectangle. Mark the rectangle lengthways into three strips, then across the strips at 2.5cm/1 inch intervals to make 30 rectangles. Prick with a fork and bake in a preheated oven at 200°C/400°F/gas 6 for 15 minutes. Remove from the oven and cut through the marked lines while still warm, discarding the excess biscuit around the edges. Transfer the biscuits to a wire rack to cool.

To finish the biscuits, break the white chocolate into pieces and melt in a heatproof bowl over a saucepan of simmering water. Use the white chocolate to sandwich the biscuits together in pairs. Leave to set; then dust lightly with cocoa powder.

Chocolate Florentines

Makes about 30   125g/4 oz/¾ cup flaked (slivered) almonds
30g/1 oz/2 tablespoons glacé (candied) cherries
45g/1½ oz/3 tablespoons unsalted butter
4 tablespoons double (heavy) cream
60g/2 oz/¼ cup caster (superfine) sugar
30g/1 oz/2 tablespoons chopped mixed peel
15g/½ oz/2 tablespoons plain (all-purpose) flour

To Decorate: 90g/3 oz/3 squares plain (dark) chocolate
90g/3 oz/3 squares white chocolate

Line two baking sheets with non-stick baking parchment. Crumble the almonds roughly into smaller flakes. Chop the glacé cherries into smaller pieces. Melt the butter in a small saucepan with the cream and sugar. Bring to the boil and remove from the heat. Stir in the almonds, cherries, mixed peel and flour. Beat together until evenly mixed.

Place teaspoonfuls of the mixture, spaced well apart, on the prepared baking sheets. Bake in a preheated oven at 180°C/350°F/gas 4 for 6–8 minutes until the mixture has spread and is turning golden around the edges. Use a lightly oiled plain biscuit (cookie) cutter to bring the edges of each biscuit towards the centre, creating neat round shapes. Transfer to a wire rack to cool. Bake any remaining mixture in the same way.

Break the plain chocolate into pieces and melt in a heatproof bowl over a saucepan of simmering water. Melt the white chocolate in the same way and keep separate. Spread the chocolate over the back of each biscuit and finish by marking wavy lines with a fork. Return to the wire rack until set.

Brandy Snap Cigars

Makes 10-12

60g/2 oz/¼ cup unsalted butter
90g/3 oz/¼ cup golden (light corn) syrup
45g/1½ oz/3 tablespoons caster (superfine) sugar
2 tablespoons cocoa powder
60g/2 oz/½ cup plain (all-purpose) flour
60g/2 oz/2 squares plain (dark) or milk chocolate to decorate

Line a large baking sheet with non-stick baking parchment. Place the butter, syrup and sugar in a small saucepan and heat gently until the butter has melted. Remove from the heat. Sift the cocoa powder and flour into the pan and stir well.

Spoon 4 teaspoonfuls of the mixture, spaced well apart, on to the prepared baking sheet and bake in a preheated oven at 190°C/375°F/gas 5 for about 5 minutes until the mixture has spread and is just turning a darker colour around the edges. Leave to cool for about 30 seconds, then peel a biscuit away from the paper and wrap around the handle of a wooden spoon. Remove from the spoon and shape the remaining biscuits. Transfer to a wire rack to cool while cooking the remaining mixture in batches.

To decorate the biscuits, break the chocolate into pieces and melt in a heatproof bowl over a pan of simmering water. Dip the ends of the biscuits in the melted chocolate; then transfer them to a sheet of greaseproof paper to set.

Cook's Tip
If the biscuits harden before you have shaped them, return them to the oven for a few moments to soften.

Left: Chocolate Florentines.

Chunky Chocolate Chip Cookies

Makes 6

90g/3 oz/3 squares plain (dark) chocolate
150g/5 oz/1¼ cups plain (all-purpose) flour
½ teaspoon bicarbonate of soda (baking soda)
75g/2½ oz/scant ½ cup light muscovado sugar
60g/2 oz/¼ cup unsalted butter or margarine
1 teaspoon vanilla essence (extract)
1 tablespoon golden (light corn) syrup
1 egg

Grease a large baking sheet lightly. Chop the chocolate into small pieces. Sift the flour and bicarbonate of soda into a bowl. Stir in the sugar.

Melt the butter or margarine in a small saucepan and add to the bowl with the vanilla essence and golden syrup. Beat the egg and measure 2 tablespoons into the bowl. Beat the ingredients together until blended, then add the chocolate pieces.

Divide the mixture into six portions. Shape each into a 'cake' and place on the prepared baking sheet, flattening each slightly. Bake in a preheated oven at 190°C/375°F/gas 5 for 15–20 minutes, until turning darker around the edges. Leave on the baking sheet for 5 minutes before transferring to a wire rack to cool completely.

Cook's Tip

These traditional American-style cookies are much larger than ordinary biscuits, although you can of course divide the mixture into smaller portions to make more cookies.

Chewy Chocolate Oat Cookies

Makes 16

125g/4 oz/1 cup self-raising flour
½ teaspoon bicarbonate of soda (baking soda)
150g/5 oz/1½ cups porridge oats
60g/2 oz/¼ cup no-need-to-soak prunes
150g/5 oz/⅔ cup unsalted butter or margarine
150g/5 oz/scant 1 cup light muscovado sugar
1 tablespoon golden (light corn) syrup
90g/3 oz/¼ cup plain (dark) or milk chocolate chips
Icing (confectioners') sugar or cocoa powder for dusting

Grease two baking sheets lightly. Sift the flour and bicarbonate of soda into a bowl. Stir in the porridge oats. Chop the prunes.

Put the butter or margarine, sugar and golden syrup in a small saucepan and heat gently until the butter has melted. Remove from the heat and add to the flour mixture, stirring until evenly combined.

Leave to cool for 20 minutes, then stir in the chocolate and prunes. Spoon tablespoonfuls of the mixture, spaced well apart, on to the prepared baking sheets. Bake in a preheated oven at 180°C/350°F/gas 4 for about 15 minutes until golden. Leave on the baking sheets for 3 minutes before transferring to a wire rack to cool completely. Serve dusted with icing sugar or cocoa powder.

Variation
Use dried apricots, dates or figs instead of the prunes.

Left: Left to right, Chunky Chocolate Chip Cookies and Chewy Chocolate Oat Cookies.

Chocolate Coffee Palmiers

Makes 25

30g/1 oz/1 square plain (dark) chocolate
60g/2 oz/¼ cup caster (superfine) sugar
1 tablespoon ground espresso coffee
or coffee powder
250g/9 oz packet puff pastry
Beaten egg to glaze

Grease 2 baking sheets lightly. Grate the chocolate finely and mix in a small bowl with half the sugar and the coffee.

Roll out the pastry on a work surface (counter), sprinkling with the remaining sugar as you roll, to an 28cm/11 inch square. Trim off the edges and brush the pastry with a little beaten egg. Sprinkle with the chocolate mixture. Roll up the pastry from one side to the centre. Roll up the other side to meet the first roll. Moisten the rolls with beaten egg and press together firmly.

Using a sharp knife, cut the roll into thin slices and transfer the pastry to the prepared baking sheets. Flatten slightly with the back of a fork, then bake in a preheated oven at 220°C/425°F/gas 7 for 10–15 minutes until golden. Transfer the biscuits to a wire rack to cool.

Variation

These simple biscuits can be transformed into delicious teatime pastries if sandwiched in pairs with cream.

Chocolate Walnut Crisps

Makes about 30

45g/1½ oz/⅓ cup walnuts
125g/4 oz/½ cup unsalted butter, softened
90g/3 oz/½ cup icing (confectioners') sugar
1 teaspoon vanilla essence (extract)
125g/4 oz/1 cup self-raising flour
2 tablespoons cocoa powder
Icing (confectioners') sugar for dusting

Grease two baking sheets lightly. Chop the walnuts fairly finely.

Above: Chocolate Peanut Shortbread.

Chocolate Peanut Shortbread

Makes 10

60g/2 oz/½ cup shelled peanuts, roughly chopped
60g/2 oz/2 squares milk chocolate
90g/3 oz/⅓ cup unsalted butter, softened
60g/2 oz/¼ cup crunchy peanut butter
60g/2 oz/¼ cup caster (superfine) sugar
175g/6 oz/1½ cups plain (all-purpose) flour
Cocoa powder or icing (confectioners') sugar for dusting

Place a 20cm/8 inch flan ring on a baking sheet and grease lightly or use a 20cm/8 inch loose-base cake tin (pan).

Cream the butter, peanut butter and sugar together until smooth. Work in the flour gradually to form a dough. Press the mixture into the flan ring or tin and flatten with the back of a spoon. Mark into 10 portions.

Chop the chocolate into small pieces and scatter with the peanuts, pressing them down lightly. Bake in a pre-heated oven at 180°C/350°F/gas 4 for 20–25 minutes until the nuts are turning golden. Remove from the oven and cut into 10 wedges along the marked lines. Leave to cool in the tin and serve dusted with cocoa powder or icing sugar.

Beat the butter and sugar together until pale and stir in the vanilla essence. Sift the flour and cocoa powder into the bowl and mix to a firm paste. Chill for about 30 minutes.

Place teaspoonfuls of the mixture on the prepared baking sheets. Flatten slightly with the back of a fork; then scatter with the chopped walnuts. Bake in a preheated oven at 180°C/350°F/gas 4 for 8–10 minutes until the mixture has spread and the nuts are turning golden. Leave on the baking sheet for 3 minutes, then transfer to a wire rack to cool. Serve dusted with icing sugar.

Chocolate Ginger Biscuits

Makes 15-20
300g/11 oz/2¾ cups plain (all-purpose) flour
30g/1 oz/¼ cup cocoa powder
1 teaspoon ground ginger
1 teaspoon ground mixed spice
1 teaspoon bicarbonate of soda
125g/4 oz/½ cup unsalted butter
175g/6 oz/¾ cup caster (superfine) sugar
4 teaspoons golden (light corn) syrup
1 egg
30g/1 oz/1 square plain (dark) chocolate

Grease two baking sheets lightly. Sift the flour, cocoa powder, ginger, mixed spice and bicarbonate of soda into a bowl. Cut the butter into small pieces and rub into the flour mixture with your fingertips.

Add the sugar, syrup and egg, and mix to a firm dough. Knead lightly until smooth. Roll out half the mixture on a lightly floured work surface (counter) and cut out shapes, using gingerbread cutters. Transfer them to the prepared baking sheets and bake in a preheated oven at 190°C/375°F/gas 5 for about 15 minutes until slightly risen. Leave on the baking sheets for 5 minutes before carefully transferring to a wire rack to cool completely. Roll out the remaining mixyure and bake in the same way.

To decorate the biscuits, break the chocolate into pieces and melt in a heatproof bowl over a saucepan of simmering water. Using a fine paintbrush, paint decorative features such as buttons and faces on to the biscuits. Leave to set.

Right: Chocolate Ginger Biscuits.

Variation

If you have not got any gingerbread cutters, use plain or novelty-shaped biscuit (cooky) cutters. After baking, these can also be painted attractively with the melted chocolate.

Miniature Chocolate Macaroons

Makes about 20

60g/2 oz/½ cup ground almonds
30g/1 oz/1 square plain (dark) chocolate
60g/2 oz/¼ cup caster (superfine) sugar
½ teaspoon vanilla or almond essence (extract)
½ teaspoon cocoa powder
1 egg white
30g/1 oz/¼ cup flaked (slivered) almonds

Line a large baking sheet with non-stick baking parchment. Toast the ground almonds lightly, watching closely as soon as they start to colour. Leave to cool. Break the chocolate into pieces and melt in a heatproof bowl over a saucepan of simmering water.

Mix the ground almonds in a bowl with the sugar, vanilla or almond essence, cocoa powder and melted chocolate. Whisk the egg white lightly and add to the bowl gradually to make a firm paste.

Place small teaspoonfuls of the mixture on the prepared baking sheet and flatten slightly. Crush the flaked almonds lightly between your fingers, then scatter them over the macaroons. Bake in a preheated oven at 200°C/400°F/gas 6 for 8–10 minutes until just firm. Remove the macaroons from the paper and transfer to a wire rack to cool.

These small cakes, generally made in slabs and cut into fingers or squares, are ideal for transporting, making perfect fillers for lunch boxes and picnics. The choice is invitingly varied from sponge-based cakes to flaky fruit bakes and crumbly shortbread slices. If you do not have the correct tin, they will not be spoiled in a similar-sized tin (pan), just keep an eye on the cooking time. When cooled, slice the traybakes and store for several days in an airtight container.

Opposite: Sticky Pear Bake.

Sticky Pear Bake

Makes 16

4 large ripe pears
150g/5 oz/⅔ cup unsalted butter, softened
30g/1 oz/1½ tablespoons light muscovado sugar
125g/4 oz/½ cup caster (superfine) sugar
125g/4 oz/¾ cup self-raising flour
2 tablespoons cocoa powder
½ teaspoon baking powder
2 eggs

Grease and line the base of a 23cm/9 in square shallow baking tin (pan) or cake tin. Peel, quarter and core the pears. Cut into thick slices.

Melt 15g/½oz/1 tablespoon of the butter in a saucepan. Add the pears and soften in the butter for 3 minutes. Arrange in a single layer in the base of the tin. Put the muscovado sugar in the pan with 2 tablespoons water. Cook, stirring continuously until the sugar has dissolved; then cook rapidly until very syrupy. Stir in another 15g/½oz/1 tablespoon of the butter until melted and then pour the syrup over the pears.

Place the remaining butter in a bowl with the caster sugar. Sift the flour, cocoa powder and baking powder into the bowl. Add the eggs and beat well until light and fluffy. Spoon over the pears and level the surface. Bake in a preheated oven at 180°C/350°F/gas 4 for about 30 minutes until risen and firm in the centre.

Leave in the tin for 5 minutes. Loosen the edges of the traybake with a knife, then invert on to a flat plate and peel away the lining paper. Leave to cool slightly and serve cut into squares.

Streusel Slices

Makes 14

125g/4 oz/4 squares plain (dark) chocolate
250g/9 oz/2¼ cups self-raising flour
1 teaspoon ground mixed (apple pie) spice
Finely grated rind of 1 lemon
175g/6 oz/¾ cup unsalted butter
150g/5 oz/scant 1 cup light muscovado sugar
60g/2 oz/½ cup ground almonds
1 egg
2 tablespoons cocoa powder
Icing (confectioners') sugar or cocoa powder for dusting

Grease a 36x11.5cm/14x4½inch loose-based rectangular flan tin (pan) lightly. Chop the chocolate into small pieces. Sift the flour and spice into a bowl. Add the lemon rind and butter, cut into small pieces. Rub the butter into the flour until the mixture begins to cling together. Add the sugar and almonds and mix until crumbly. Reserve a third of the mixture and beat the egg into the remainder. Mix to a dough.

Press the dough into the prepared tin. Stir the chopped chocolate and cocoa powder into the reserved crumble mixture. Scatter over the base in an even layer. Bake the Streusel in a preheated oven at 180°C/350°F/gas 4 for 35–40 minutes until slightly risen and turning golden.

Leave to cool slightly in the tin, then cut into slices and transfer to a wire rack. Serve dusted with icing sugar or cocoa powder.

Right: Left to right: Warm Cheesecake Squares and Apple and Chocolate Puffs.

Chocolate Espresso Squares

Makes 15

175g/6 oz/¾ cup margarine, softened
175g/6 oz/¾ cup caster (superfine) sugar
175g/6 oz/1½ cups self-raising flour
30g/1 oz/¼ cup cocoa powder
1 teaspoon baking powder
4 teaspoons espresso coffee or coffee powder
3 eggs
1 tablespoon milk
150g/5 oz/1¼ cups walnut pieces

Icing:

125g/4 oz/4 squares plain (dark) chocolate
3 tablespoons golden (light corn) syrup
30g/1 oz/2 tablespoons unsalted butter

Grease and line a 33x23cm/13x9 inch Swiss (jelly) roll tin (pan). Put the margarine and sugar in a bowl. Sift the flour, cocoa powder and coffee powder into the bowl. Add the eggs, and beat with an electric whisk until light and fluffy. Stir in the milk. Spread the mixture into the prepared tin and level the surface. Scatter with the walnut pieces. Bake in a preheated oven at 170°C/325°F/ gas 3 for about 25 minutes until risen and just firm to the touch.

To make the icing, break the chocolate into pieces and place in a heavy-based saucepan with the syrup, butter and 3 tablespoons water. Heat gently, stirring continuously until the chocolate is melted and the mixture is smooth. Spoon over the cake; then cut into squares.

Chocolate Pecan Slices

Makes 10

90g/3 oz/¾ cup self-raising flour
60g/2 oz/¼ cup unsalted butter
30g/1 oz/2 tablespoons light muscovado sugar
125g/4 oz/1 cup pecan nuts

To Finish:

½ teaspoon cornflour (cornstarch)
5 tablespoons orange juice
125ml/4 fl oz/½ cup maple syrup
60g/2 oz/2 squares plain (dark) chocolate

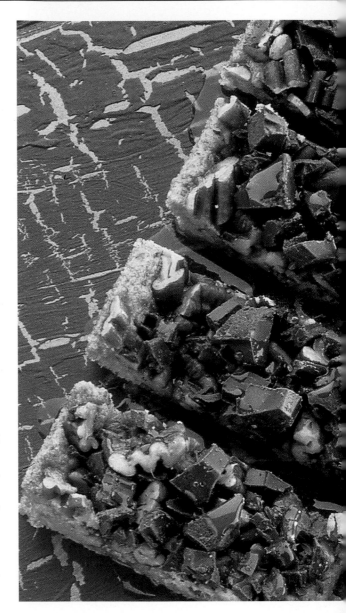

Grease the base and sides of a 15cm/6 inch square loose-base cake tin (pan) lightly.

Sift the flour into a bowl. Cut the butter into small pieces and rub into the flour with your fingertips. Stir in the sugar and mix to a firm dough. Press into the prepared tin and level with the back of a teaspoon. Chop the pecan nuts very lightly and scatter over the surface. Bake in a preheated oven at 180°C/350°F/gas 4 for about 20 minutes until slightly risen and beginning to colour around the edges.

Blend the cornflour with a little of the orange juice in a small saucepan. Blend in the remaining orange juice and the maple syrup. Cook over a moderate heat, stirring continuously, until the mixture is clear and thickened. Leave to cool slightly; then brush the syrup over the pecan base. Leave to cool completely. Remove the sides of the tin. Chop the chocolate and scatter over the cake. Cut the cake into 10 wedges.

Variation
For a mild coffee flavouring, add 1 teaspoon coffee powder to the flour. If liked, substitute walnuts for the pecans.

Warm Cheesecake Squares

| Makes 16 | 125g/4 oz digestive biscuits (graham crackers) |
| | 60g/2 oz/½ cup unsalted butter |

Cheesecake:	60g/2 oz/½ cup hazelnuts
	125g/4 oz/4 squares plain (dark) chocolate
	225g/8 oz/1 cup cottage cheese
	2 eggs
	125g/4 oz/½ cup caster (superfine) sugar
	150ml/¼ pint/⅔ cup double (heavy) cream
	30g/1 oz/¼ cup cocoa powder
	Icing (confectioners') sugar for dusting

Grease the sides of a 20cm/8 inch square shallow baking tin (pan) or cake tin. Place the biscuits in a thick plastic bag and crush with a rolling pin. Melt the butter in a saucepan. Add the biscuits, stirring until evenly coated. Turn into the prepared tin and press down lightly.

To make the cheesecake, chop the nuts roughly and break the chocolate into pieces. Press the cottage cheese through a sieve (strainer) into a bowl. Separate the eggs and add the yolks to the bowl with the sugar, cream and cocoa powder. Beat well until smooth; then stir in the nuts and chopped chocolate.

Whisk the egg whites until stiff; then fold a quarter into the chocolate mixture, using a large metal spoon. Fold in the remainder carefully. Spoon into the tin and level the surface. Bake in a preheated oven at 170°C/325°F/gas 3 for about 1½ hours until just firm. Leave to cool slightly, then cut into squares and serve warm, dusted with icing sugar.

Left: Chocolate Pecan Slices.

Millionaire's Shortbread

Makes 12

90g/3 oz/¾ cup plain (all-purpose) flour
60g/2 oz/¼ cup unsalted butter
30g/1 oz/2 tablespoons caster (superfine) sugar

Topping:

60g/2 oz/¼ cup unsalted butter
60g/2 oz/¼ cup caster (superfine) sugar
397g/14 oz can sweetened condensed milk
150g/5 oz/5 squares plain (dark) chocolate

Grease an 18cm/7 inch square cake tin (pan) lightly. Sift the flour into a bowl. Cut the butter into small pieces and rub into the flour with your fingertips. Add the sugar and mix to a firm dough. Press the mixture into the prepared tin and level with the back of a spoon. Bake in a preheated oven at 180°C/350°F/gas 4 for about 20 minutes, or until just beginning to colour around the edges. Leave to cool in the tin.

To make the caramel topping, place the butter, sugar and condensed milk in a heavy-based saucepan. Heat gently, stirring continuously, until the sugar has dissolved. Bring to the boil, then reduce the heat and simmer for about 5 minutes until slightly thickened. Pour over the shortbread base and leave to cool completely.

Break the chocolate into pieces and melt in a heatproof bowl over a saucepan of simmering water. Remove from the heat and stir lightly. Pour the chocolate over the caramel and spread to the edges of the tin. Chill until set. To serve the shortbread, cut into pieces and remove from the tin carefully.

Right: Sticky Flapjacks.

Cook's Tip
Serve the shortbread in small portions. It is delicious but extremely rich!

Sticky Flapjacks

Makes 20

125g/4 oz/4 squares plain (dark) chocolate
175g/6 oz/¾ cup unsalted butter or margarine
125g/4 oz/½ cup caster (superfine) sugar
125g/4 oz/⅔ cup dark muscovado sugar
125g/4 oz/⅓ cup golden (light corn) syrup
425g/15 oz/4½ cups porridge oats

Grease a 25x18cm/10x7 inch shallow baking tin (pan) lightly. Chop the chocolate roughly.

Put the butter or margarine into a heavy-based sauce-pan with both sugars and the syrup. Cook over a moderate heat until the sugar has melted. Remove from the heat and beat in the porridge oats; then add the chopped chocolate.

Spoon the mixture into the prepared tin, spreading into the corners and levelling with the back of a teaspoon. Bake in a preheated oven at 180°C/350°F/gas 4 for about 25 minutes until slightly risen and colouring around the edges. Leave to cool slightly in the tin; then mark into 20 fingers.

Cook's Tip
If you prefer, pack the mixture into the tin and scatter the chopped chocolate on top.

Apple and Chocolate Puffs

Makes 10

900g/2 lb cooking apples
1 tablespoon lemon juice
200g/7 oz/7 squares plain (dark) chocolate
½ teaspoon ground cinnamon
30g/1 oz/2 tablespoons unsalted butter
450g/1 lb puff pastry
30g/1 oz/2 tablespoons caster (superfine) sugar
60g/2 oz/⅓ cup sultanas (golden raisins)
Beaten egg to glaze
Caster (superfine) sugar to sprinkle

Grease a 33x23cm/13x9 inch Swiss (jelly) roll tin (pan) lightly. Peel, quarter and core the apples. Cut into fairly thick slices and place in a bowl of cold water with the lemon juice.

Break the chocolate into pieces and put in a heatproof bowl with the cinnamon and butter. Melt over a saucepan of simmering water.

Halve the pastry and roll out one half thinly on a floured work surface (counter) to a rectangle slightly larger than the tin. Lay in the tin, pressing the pastry up the sides. Drain the apples thoroughly and toss in the sugar. Scatter the apples in an even layer over the pastry. Sprinkle with the sultanas. Stir the chocolate mixture lightly and place small spoonfuls over the apples until partially covered. Brush the edges of the pastry with a little beaten egg.

Roll out the remaining pastry and lay over the filling, pressing the edges of the pastry together firmly to seal. Brush with beaten egg; then mark decorative diagonal lines over the pastry. Sprinkle with sugar and bake in a preheated oven at 220°C/425°F/gas 7 for about 25 minutes until risen and golden.

Leave to cool slightly; then serve warm or cold, cut into rectangles.

Variation
Ripe pears make an equally good alternative to the apples. Toss them in half the quantity of caster (superfine) sugar to allow for their sweeter flavour.

White Chocolate Fingers

Makes 16

175g/6 oz ginger snap biscuits (cookies)
90g/3 oz/⅓ cup unsalted butter
125g/4 oz/4 squares white chocolate
30g/1 oz/⅓ cup desiccated (shredded) coconut

Topping:

90g/3 oz /3 squares white chocolate
50g/2 oz/¼ cup unsalted butter or margarine, softened
60g/2 oz/¼ cup caster (superfine) sugar
90g/3 oz/¾ cup self-raising flour
30g/1 oz/½ cup desiccated (shredded) coconut
Finely grated rind of 1 lemon
1 teaspoon ground ginger
2 tablespoons milk
90g/3 oz/3 squares white chocolate to decorate

To make the base, place the biscuits in a thick plastic bag and crush with a rolling pin. Melt the butter and mix with the biscuits. Spread into the base of a 25x18cm/10x7 inch shallow baking tin (pan). Press down gently with the back of a spoon.

Break the white chocolate into pieces and melt in a heatproof bowl over a saucepan of simmering water. Stir in the coconut and spread over the base. Chill.

To make the topping, break the white chocolate into pieces and melt as above. Beat the butter or margarine and sugar together until light and fluffy. Add the flour, coconut, lemon rind, ginger, milk and melted chocolate, and beat until smooth. Spread over the prepared base and bake in a preheated oven at 190°C/375°F/gas 5 for about 25 minutes until slightly risen and golden. Leave to cool slightly; then cut into fingers. Transfer to a wire rack to cool completely.

To decorate, melt the white chocolate as above and place in a piping bag fitted with a writing tube (tip). Use to drizzle lines over the fingers. Leave until set.

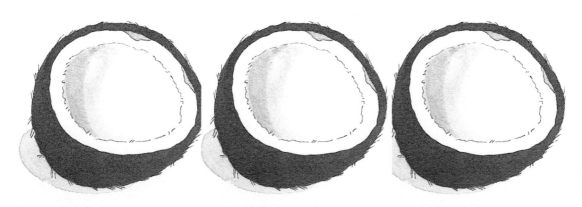

Chocolate is a favourite flavouring for many classic 'teatime' cakes and many are included in this chapter. Pretty meringues, tartlets and eclairs use a subtle chocolate flavouring, while the brownies, muffins, cup cakes and strudels use chocolate in more robust quantities.

For maximum enjoyment, some of the small cakes should be served warm. The croissants, oozing chocolate sauce and almond paste, make an excellent mid-morning treat while the Chocolate and Orange Drop Scones (p.51), dripping in orange butter, are perfect as a teatime snack. Likewise, the quick and easy Chocolate Cinnamon Doughnuts (p.54) are delicious eaten freshly fried, although any leftovers will reheat in a moderate oven.

Previous page: Left to right, White Chocolate Strawberry Tartlets, Chocolate Whirls (p.50) and Chocolate and Orange Eclairs.

White Chocolate and Strawberry Tartlets

Makes 8	175g/6 oz/1½ cups plain (all-purpose) flour
	90g/3 oz/⅓ cup unsalted butter
	3 egg yolks
	30g/1 oz/2 tablespoons caster (superfine) sugar
Filling:	125g/4 oz/4 squares white chocolate
	250ml/8 fl oz/1 cup double (heavy) cream
To Decorate:	225g/8 oz/1½ cups strawberries
	4 tablespoons redcurrant jelly
	White chocolate caraque (p.7)

Sift the flour into a bowl. Cut the butter into small pieces, and rub into the flour with your fingertips. Stir in the egg yolks and sugar, and mix to a firm dough, adding a few drops of water if the mixture is too dry. Knead lightly until smooth and chill for 30 minutes.

Roll out the pastry on a lightly floured work surface (counter). Cut into eight portions and use to line eight individual flan tins (pans), about 9cm/3½ inches in diameter. Line each tin with greaseproof paper (baking parchment) and fill with baking beans. Bake in a preheated oven at 190°C/375°F/gas 5 for 15 minutes until turning golden around the edges. Remove the beans and paper, and return to the oven for a further 5 minutes. Leave to cool.

To make the filling, break the chocolate into pieces. Pour half the cream into a saucepan and bring just to the boil. Remove from the heat and stir in the chocolate until it has melted. Spoon the mixture into a bowl and stir in the remaining cream. Leave to cool; then whisk until it is just peaking. Spread the chocolate cream into the tartlet cases.

To decorate the tartlets, cut the strawberries into thin slices and arrange over the filling. Melt the redcurrant jelly in a saucepan with 1 tablespoon water. Leave to cool until beginning to thicken; then use to glaze the tartlets. Decorate with white chocolate caraque and chill until ready to serve.

Chocolate and Orange Eclairs

Makes about 16	75g/2½oz/½ cup
	plus 2 tablespoons plain (all-purpose) flour
	60g/2 oz/¼ cup unsalted butter
	2 eggs
Filling:	150ml/¼ pint/⅔ cup double (heavy) cream
	Finely grated rind of ½ orange
	1 teaspoon icing (confectioners') sugar
To Decorate:	175g/6 oz/6 squares plain (dark) chocolate
	60g/2 oz/¼ cup icing (confectioners') sugar
	1 teaspoon orange juice

Grease two baking sheets lightly and moisten them. Sift the flour into a bowl. Place the butter in a small pan with 150ml/¼ pint/⅔ cup water and heat gently until the butter has melted. Bring to the boil, remove from the heat and add the flour immediately. Beat thoroughly with a wooden spoon. Continue beating over the heat until the mixture is smooth and comes away cleanly from the sides of the pan. Leave to cool for 2 minutes.

Beat the eggs and beat into the flour mixture gradually, a little at a time until the mixture is glossy. Place in a piping bag fitted with a 1cm/½ inch plain tube (tip) and pipe fingers, about 6cm/2½ inches long on to the baking sheets.

Bake in a preheated oven at 200°C/400°F/gas 6 for 20–25 minutes until well risen and golden. Reduce the oven temperature to 180°C/350°F/gas 4. Make a slit along the side of each éclair and return to the oven for a further 5 minutes to dry out the centres. Transfer to a wire rack to cool.

To make the filling, whisk the cream, orange rind and icing sugar until it is just peaking. Spoon or pipe the cream into the eclairs.

To decorate the éclairs, break the chocolate into pieces and melt in a heatproof bowl over a saucepan of simmering water. Blend the icing sugar with enough orange juice to give the consistency of pouring cream. Spread a little chocolate over each éclair, then spoon a little of the orange icing over the chocolate. Using the tip of a cocktail stick (toothpick), swirl the icing into the chocolate.

Chocolate Whirls

Makes 12	200g/7 oz/scant 1 cup unsalted butter, softened
	60g/2 oz/⅓ cup icing (confectioners') sugar
	200g/7 oz/1¾ cups plain (all-purpose) flour
	30g/1 oz/¼ cup cocoa powder
	½ teaspoon baking powder
To Decorate:	90g/3 oz/3 squares plain (dark) chocolate
	Cocoa powder for dusting

Line a 12-section tartlet tin (pan) with paper cases. Beat the butter and icing sugar together until pale and creamy. Sift the flour, cocoa powder and baking powder into the bowl and beat in to make a smooth, soft paste.

Spoon the mixture into a large piping bag fitted with a large star tube (tip). Pile swirls into the centres of the cases, leaving a small cavity in the centre. Bake in a preheated oven at 190°C/375°F/gas 5 for 15–20 minutes until risen; then transfer to a wire rack to cool.

To decorate, break the chocolate into pieces and melt in a heatproof bowl over a saucepan of simmering water. Spoon a little into the centre of each whirl. Leave to set; then serve dusted with cocoa powder.

Cook's Tip
If you do not have a large bag and tube (tip), spoon the mixture into the cases and make a cavity with the back of a teaspoon before baking.

Right: Chocolate and Orange Drop Scones.

Chocolate and Orange Drop Scones

Serves 6

125g/4 oz/4 squares plain (dark) or milk chocolate
125g/4 oz/1 cup self-raising flour
½ teaspoon baking powder
2 tablespoons caster (superfine) sugar
1 egg
200ml/7 fl oz/scant 1 cup milk
Oil for shallow-frying

Orange Butter:

90g/3 oz/⅓ cup unsalted butter, softened
2 tablespoons icing (confectioners') sugar
Finely grated rind of 1 orange

To make the orange butter, place the butter, icing sugar and orange rind in a bowl with 1 teaspoon hot water and beat until light and fluffy. Transfer to a small serving dish and chill.

To make the scones, cut the chocolate into small pieces. Sift the flour and baking powder into a bowl and stir in the sugar. Make a well in the centre and add the egg and a little of the milk. Whisk the mixture to a batter; then beat in the remaining milk and the chocolate pieces.

Heat a little oil in a frying pan (skillet) or griddle. Add dessertspoonfuls of the batter and fry gently until turning golden on underside. Flip over the scones and fry again until golden. Drain and keep warm while cooking the remainder.

Serve the drop scones warm, accompanied by the orange butter.

Chocolate Almond Brownies

Makes 18

175g/6 oz/1½ cups blanched almonds
450g/1 lb plain (dark) chocolate
225g/8 oz/1 cup unsalted butter or margarine, softened
3 eggs
225g/8 oz/1⅓ cups light muscovado sugar
90g/3 oz/¾ cup self-raising flour
1 teaspoon almond essence (extract)

Grease and line a 25x18cm/10x7 inch shallow baking tin (pan). Chop the almonds very roughly and lightly toast them. Chop 125g/4 oz/4 squares of the chocolate finely and reserve.

Break the remaining chocolate into pieces and put in a heatproof bowl with the butter or margarine. Melt over a saucepan of simmering water.

Beat together the eggs and sugar in a bowl. Beat in the melted chocolate mixture gradually. Sift the flour over the mixture and fold in with the almonds, almond essence and chopped chocolate.

Spoon the mixture into the prepared tin and bake in a preheated oven at 190°C/375°F/gas 5 for about 35 minutes until the surface is crusty and feels only just firm. Leave to cool in the tin, then turn out and cut into portions.

Cook's Tip
When cooked the cake should be crusty on the surface but feel quite soft underneath. This cools to a deliciously moist, gooey texture.

Right: Chocolate Almond Brownies.

Chocolate Cup Cakes

Makes 12

90g/3 oz/3 squares milk chocolate
60g/2 oz/¼ cup soft margarine
60g/2 oz/¼ cup caster (superfine) sugar
1 egg
45g/1½ oz/⅓ cup self-raising flour
2 tablespoons cocoa powder

Icing:

175g/6 oz/6 squares plain (dark) chocolate
3 tablespoons orange juice
90g/3 oz/½ cup icing (confectioners') sugar

Line a 12-section tartlet tin (pan) with paper cases. Chop the milk chocolate roughly.

Place the margarine, sugar, egg, flour and cocoa powder in a bowl and beat until smooth and paler in colour. Stir in the chopped chocolate. Divide the mixture between the paper cases and bake in a preheated oven at 180°C/350°F/gas 4 for about 10 minutes until risen and just firm. Leave to cool.

To make the icing, break the chocolate into pieces and put in a heatproof bowl with the orange juice. Rest the bowl over a saucepan of simmering water and leave until melted. Stir in the icing sugar.

Cut any excess domes off the chocolate cakes; then spread them with the chocolate icing. Leave until set.

Variation

For two-tone chocolate cup cakes, substitute white chocolate for the plain in the icing.

Chocolate Cinnamon Doughnuts

Makes 8

125g/4 oz/4 squares plain (dark) chocolate
15g/½oz/1 tablespoon unsalted butter
280g/9½oz packet bread mix
½ teaspoon ground cinnamon
1 tablespoon caster (superfine) sugar

To Finish:

Oil for deep-frying
60g/2 oz/¼ cup caster (superfine) sugar
2 teaspoons ground cinnamon

Break the chocolate into pieces and place in a heatproof bowl with the butter. Leave until melted. Place the bread mix and cinnamon in a bowl and make up with milk or water following the packet directions. Knead and leave to rise in a warm place until doubled in size.

Put the dough on a lightly floured work surface (counter) and knead lightly. Divide into eight portions. Roll out one piece to a round, about 10cm/4inches in diameter. Place a spoonful of the chocolate mixture in the centre. Bring the edges of the dough up around the chocolate and pinch together to enclose it. Place on a lightly greased baking sheet. Shape the remaining doughnuts in the same way. Cover them loosely with oiled cling film (plastic wrap) and leave to rise again until doubled in size.

Heat the oil in a deep-frying pan until a little dough sizzles on the surface. Add 2–3 doughnuts to the pan and fry for about 3 minutes until puffed and golden. Remove with a slotted spoon and drain on paper towels. Mix the sugar and cinnamon on a plate and use to coat the doughnuts. Serve freshly made.

Cook's Tip
Avoid letting the oil get too hot, or the doughnuts will be crusty and overbrowned on the surface while still raw in the centre.

Mini Chocolate Strudels

Makes 9

125g/4 oz/4 squares plain (dark) chocolate
60g/2 oz/½ cup walnuts
60g/2 oz/½ cup raisins
½ teaspoon ground mixed (apple pie) spice
45g/1½ oz/3 tablespoons unsalted butter
3 large sheets filo pastry
Cocoa powder for dusting

Grease a baking sheet lightly. Break the chocolate into pieces and melt in a heatproof bowl over a saucepan of simmering water. Chop the walnuts roughly and mix with the chocolate, raisins and mixed spice.

Melt the butter. Cut the pastry sheets widthways into three, to give nine rectangles. Brush over each with the melted butter. Spoon the chocolate down the centre of each rectangle. Fold the long edges over the filling; then roll up each to make small strudels.

Place with the joins underneath on the baking sheet and brush with the remaining butter. Bake in a preheated oven at 200°C/400°F/gas 6 for about 10 minutes until golden. Serve warm or cold, dusted with cocoa powder.

Left: Chocolate Cinnamon Doughnuts.

Double Chocolate Chip Muffins

Makes 12

175g/6 oz/6 squares plain (dark) chocolate
350g/12 oz/3 cups self-raising flour
1 tablespoon baking powder
90g/3 oz/¾ cup cocoa powder
90g/3 oz/½ cup light muscovado sugar
90g/3 oz/¾ cup plain (dark) chocolate chips
90g/3 oz/¾ cup white chocolate chips
375ml/13 fl oz/1¾ cups milk
6 tablespoons vegetable oil
2 teaspoons vanilla essence (extract)
1 egg
1 egg yolk

Line a 12-section muffin tin (pan) with paper muffin cases. Break the chocolate into pieces and melt in a heat-proof bowl over a saucepan of simmering water.

Sift the flour, baking powder and cocoa powder into a bowl. Stir in the sugar and chocolate chips. Beat together the milk, oil, vanilla essence, egg and egg yolk. Add to the bowl with the melted chocolate and fold in gently until the ingredients are just combined.

Spoon the mixture into the paper cases, piling it up in the centre. Bake in a preheated oven at 220°C/425°F/gas 7 for 20 minutes until well risen and just firm. Transfer to a wire rack to cool.

Cook's Tip

Muffin tins and cases are slightly larger than ordinary tartlet ones. If you do not have any, use the smaller size and bake the mixture in two batches.

Chocolate Frangipane Croissants

Makes 6

6 small croissants
125g/4 oz/4 squares plain (dark) chocolate
30g/1 oz/2 tablespoons unsalted butter
90g/3 oz almond paste
Icing (confectioners') sugar for dusting

Halve each croissant and place the bases on a baking sheet. Break the chocolate into pieces and place in a heatproof bowl with the butter. Rest over a saucepan of simmering water and leave until melted. Cut the almond paste into thin slices.

Arrange the almond paste slices over the croissant bases; then spoon over the chocolate mixture. Replace the croissant tops. Warm in a preheated oven at 180°C/350°F/gas 4 for 5–10 minutes and serve dusted with icing sugar.

Left: Chocolate Frangipane Croissants.

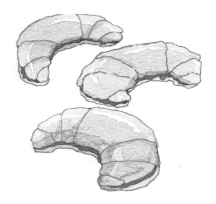

Chocolate Meringue Pairs

Makes 12-14

4 egg whites
225g/8 oz/1 cup caster (superfine) sugar
2 tablespoons cocoa powder
4 tablespoons coarse sugar or coffee sugar crystals
150ml/¼ pint/⅔ cup double (heavy) cream to decorate

Line two baking sheets with non-stick baking parchment. Whisk the egg whites until stiff. Whisk in half the sugar gradually, a tablespoon at a time. Sift the cocoa powder over the meringue and whisk in. Whisk in the remaining sugar gradually until the meringue is stiff and glossy.

Place dessertspoonfuls of the meringue, spaced slightly apart, on the prepared baking sheets. Crush the sugar lightly if it is very coarse and sprinkle over the meringues. Bake in a preheated oven at 120°C/250°F/gas ½ for 1–1½ hours until the meringues are crisp. Remove from the oven and peel away the paper.

Whip the cream lightly until it is just peaking. Sandwich together pairs of meringues by spooning or piping the cream to secure.

Variation
Adding some cocoa powder makes these meringues mildly 'chocolatey'. For a richer flavour sandwich the meringues with chocolate ganache. Heat 150ml/¼ pint/⅔ cup double (heavy) cream in a pan; then stir in 150g/5 oz/5 squares plain (dark) chocolate until melted. When cooled, beat the mixture until it is peaking.

Choose a chocolate cake for a birthday celebration and it will undoubtedly be a winner. In this chapter there is a simple Birthday Parcel Cake (p.62), attractively finished with ribbon ties, or a stunning chocolate box which you can fill with fresh cream truffles or a selection of chocolates. Either cake will delight the recipient, regardless of age.

A classic requirement on the Christmas table is the chocolate log, Buche de Noël (p.70), a light rolled sponge, filled with cream and lavishly spread with chocolate ganache. Sugar-dusted chocolate curls make a simple, but effective, decoration for this mouthwatering centrepiece.

Next page: Left to right, Chocolate Truffle Box (p.63) and Birthday Parcel Cake (p.63).

Birthday Parcel Cake

Serves 20	175g/6 oz/¾ cup soft margarine
	175g/6 oz/¾ cup caster (superfine) sugar
	3 eggs
	160g/5½ oz/1⅓ cups self-raising flour
	2 tablespoons cocoa powder
	1 teaspoon baking powder
	5 tablespoons Amaretto liqueur or orange-flavoured liqueur
	125g/4 oz/4 squares plain (dark) chocolate
	5 tablespoons double (heavy) cream
To Decorate:	3 tablespoons apricot jam
	675g/1½ lb white marzipan (almond paste)
	175g/6 oz/6 squares bitter (semisweet) chocolate
	2 tablespoons golden (light corn) syrup
	1 egg white
	450g/1lb icing (confectioners') sugar
	Cornflour (cornstarch) for dusting
	Ribbons

Grease and line a 25x18cm/10x7 inch shallow baking tin (pan). Place the margarine, sugar and eggs in a bowl. Sift the flour, cocoa powder and baking powder into the bowl. Beat well with an electric whisk until paler in colour and creamy. Turn into the prepared tin and level the surface. Bake in a preheated oven at 170°C/325°F/gas 3 for about 35–40 minutes until risen and just firm to the touch. Transfer to a wire rack and leave to cool.

Cut off any excess dome from the centre of the cake; then cut widthways into three equal pieces. Drizzle the cakes with the liqueur.

Break the chocolate into pieces and place in a small heavy-based saucepan with the cream. Heat gently until the chocolate has melted; then transfer to a bowl. Leave to cool; then whisk until the mixture is just peaking. Spread over two of the cakes and sandwich them together on a serving plate.

Melt the apricot jam and press through a sieve (strainer) into a small bowl. Brush the jam over the top and sides of the cake. Knead the almond paste lightly and then roll it out and use to cover the top and sides of the cake.

Break the bitter chocolate into pieces and place in a heatproof bowl with the golden syrup. Place over a saucepan of simmering water and leave until melted. Remove from the heat and cool slightly. Add the egg white and a little of the icing sugar. Beat with an electric whisk until smooth, adding more icing sugar gradually. When too stiff to stir, turn the mixture out on to the work surface (counter) and knead in more icing sugar to make a stiff paste. Roll out a quarter on a surface dusted with icing sugar and use to cover the top of the cake. Use the remainder to cover the sides. Using hands dusted with cornflour, smooth the icing to eliminate creases. Leave in a cool place to harden. Decorate the cake with ribbons to resemble a parcel.

Cook's Tip

This makes a perfect cake for any 'chocoholic' celebrating a birthday, and can be finished with as many ribbons as you think suitable. The chocolate icing is rather like ordinary 'ready-to-roll' icing to work with, but has a slightly softer texture when warm. If left to cool it sets fairly hard but can be softened by kneading or popping it into a microwave briefly.

Chocolate Truffle Box

Serves 16

30g/1 oz/2 tablespoons unsalted butter
3 eggs
90g/3 oz/⅓ cup caster (superfine) sugar
75g/2½ oz/½ cup plus 2 tablespoons plain (all-purpose) flour
2 tablespoons cocoa powder

To Decorate:

450ml/¾ pint/2 cups double (heavy) cream
1 tablespoon icing (confectioners') sugar
3 tablespoons brandy, rum or orange-flavoured liqueur
200g/7 oz/7 squares plain (dark) chocolate
25 bought or home-made chocolate truffles
Paper sweet (candy) cases
Ribbon (optional)

Grease the base and sides of an 18cm/7 inch square cake tin (pan). Melt the butter and reserve. Place the eggs and sugar in a large heatproof bowl over a saucepan of simmering water. Using an electric whisk beat the mixture until it leaves a trail when the whisk is lifted.

Remove from the heat and continue whisking until cooled. Sift half the flour and cocoa powder over the mixture. Drizzle the melted butter around the edges of the bowl. Using a large metal spoon fold in the flour and butter carefully. Sift over the remaining flour and cocoa powder, and fold in. Turn into the prepared tin and bake in a preheated oven at 180°C/350°F/gas 4 for 20–25 minutes until risen and just firm to the touch. Leave to cool.

To decorate the cake, place the cream, sugar and liqueur in a bowl and whisk until it is just peaking. Split the cake in half horizontally and sandwich together with a little of the whipped cream. Spread the top and sides of the cake with the remaining whipped cream.

Break the chocolate into pieces and melt in a heatproof bowl over a saucepan of simmering water. Crumple a sheet of foil lightly and then completely flatten it so that foil retains some creases. Cut the foil into a 24x19cm/9½x7½ inch rectangle. Spread the melted chocolate over the foil to within 5mm/¼ inch of the edges. Leave to set.

When completely set, trim the rectangle to 23x18cm/ 9x7 inches; then cut widthways into four equal strips. Peel the foil away carefully from the chocolate and position one strip on each side of the cake so that the corners meet. Place the truffles in paper sweet cases and arrange on top of the cake. Chill until ready to serve, and decorate, if liked, with a ribbon.

Easter Celebration Gâteau

Serves 20

250ml/8 fl oz/1 cup milk
1 tablespoon white wine vinegar
125g/4oz/4 squares bitter (semisweet) chocolate
125g/4 oz/½ cup soft margarine
225g/8 oz/1 cup caster (superfine) sugar
2 eggs
300g/11 oz/2¾ cups self-raising flour
1 teaspoon baking powder
2 tablespoons cocoa powder
2 teaspoons ground mixed spice
125g/4 oz/⅔ cup mixed dried fruit

To Decorate:
125g/4 oz/½ cup unsalted butter, softened
225g/8 oz/1⅓ cups icing (confectioners') sugar
30g/1 oz/¼ cup cocoa powder
Double quantity chocolate modelling paste (p.7)
About 250g/9 oz miniature chocolate eggs
Ribbon (optional)

Grease and line an 18cm/7 inch round cake tin (pan). Mix the milk with the vinegar. Break up the chocolate and melt in a heatproof bowl over a saucepan of simmering water.

Put the margarine, sugar and eggs into a bowl. Sift the flour, baking powder, cocoa powder and mixed spice into the bowl. Add half the milk and beat until the mixture is smooth and paler in colour. Add the remaining milk, the melted chocolate and dried fruit and mix until evenly combined. Turn into the prepared tin and level the surface.

Opposite: Easter Celebration Gâteau.

Bake in a preheated oven at 170°C/325°F/gas 3 for 1¼–1½ hours until a skewer, inserted into the centre, comes out clean. Leave to cool.

To decorate the cake, beat together the butter, icing sugar and cocoa powder with 2 teaspoons hot water until smooth and creamy. Split the cake in half horizontally and sandwich with a little of the buttercream. Place on a serving plate. Spread the remaining buttercream over the top and sides.

Knead a little of the modelling paste lightly and roll out to a strip, slightly deeper than the cake and about 18cm/6inches long. Gather up the strip slightly and secure loosely to the side of the cake. Make and secure more strips until the sides are completely covered. Pile the chocolate eggs into the centre of the cake. Keep the cake in a cool place until needed. If liked, finish the sides of the cake with ribbon.

Cook's Tip
Chocolate mini eggs often come wrapped in colourful foil. If liked, leave some of the eggs in their wrappers, matching the colours with the decorative ribbon.

White Chocolate Gâteau

Serves 16

225g/8 oz/1 cup margarine, softened
225g/8 oz/1 cup caster (superfine) sugar
Finely grated rind of 1 orange
4 eggs
225g/8 oz/2 cups self-raising flour
1 teaspoon baking powder
1 tablespoon milk
6 tablespoons Cointreau

Filling:

125g/4 oz/¾ cup strawberries
125g/4 oz/¾ cup raspberries
2 teaspoons caster (superfine) sugar
150 ml/¼ pint/⅔ cup double (heavy) cream

To Decorate:

200g/7 oz/7 squares white chocolate
300ml/½ pint/1¼ cups double (heavy) cream
White chocolate caraque, (p.7)
Cocoa powder or icing (confectioners') sugar for dusting

Grease and base-line two 20cm/8 inch sandwich tins (layer pans). Place the margarine, sugar, orange rind and eggs in a bowl. Sift the flour and baking powder into the bowl and beat well until light and fluffy. Beat in the milk. Bake in a preheated oven at 170°C/325°F/gas 3 for 25–30 minutes until risen and just firm to the touch. Transfer to a wire rack to cool; then drizzle the sponges with the Cointreau.

Opposite: White Chocolate Gâteau.

Next page: Buche de Noël.

To make the filling, slice the strawberries roughly and toss in a bowl with the raspberries and sugar. Whip the cream lightly. Place one cake on a serving plate and spread with the cream. Scatter with the fruit and cover with the remaining cake.

For the decoration, break the chocolate into pieces. Bring the cream to the boil in a small pan. Stir in the chocolate until it has melted. Transfer to a bowl and cool slightly. Beat the mixture until just peaking; then swirl over the top and sides of the cake.

Press white chocolate caraque gently over the top and sides, and dust lightly with cocoa powder. Chill until ready to serve.

Buche de Noël

Serves 10

3 eggs

90g/3 oz/⅓ cup caster (superfine) sugar, plus extra for sprinkling

60g/2 oz/½ cup plain (all-purpose) flour

2 tablespoons cocoa powder

Filling:

90g/3 oz/3 squares milk chocolate

150ml/¼ pint/⅔ cup double (heavy) cream

2 tablespoons brandy or rum

To Decorate:

225g/8 oz/8 squares plain (dark) chocolate

150ml/¼ pint/⅔ cup double (heavy) cream

30g/1 oz/1 square white chocolate

Chocolate caraque, (p.7)

Sprigs of holly

Icing (confectioners') sugar for dusting

Grease and line a 33x23cm/13x9 inch Swiss (jelly) roll tin (pan). Place the eggs and sugar in a large heatproof bowl, set over a saucepan of simmering water, and beat with an electric whisk until the mixture leaves a trail when the whisk is lifted from the bowl. Remove from the heat and whisk until cooled. Sift the flour and cocoa powder into the bowl and fold in using a large metal spoon. Turn into the prepared tin and smooth the mixture gently into the corners. Bake in a preheated oven at 200°C/400°F/gas 6 for 12–15 minutes until just firm to the touch.

Sprinkle a clean sheet of greaseproof with caster sugar and invert the cake on to it. Peel away the lining paper and then roll the cake up in the clean paper. Leave to cool.

To make the filling, chop the milk chocolate finely. Whisk the cream and brandy or rum until just peaking and

then fold in the chocolate. Unroll the cake carefully and spread with the filling. Roll the cake up again and transfer to a cake board or plate. Cut a thick diagonal slice off one end and attach to one side.

To decorate, break the plain chocolate into pieces. Bring the cream to the boil in a small pan. Remove from the heat and stir in the chocolate until it has melted. Transfer to a bowl and leave to cool.

Whip the chocolate cream lightly until peaking and then spread all over the roulade, swirling attractively with a palette knife. Melt the white chocolate and place in a piping bag fitted with a writing tube (tip). Use to pile spirals at the ends of the log. Lay the chocolate caraque decoratively over the log and decorate with holly sprigs. Dust generously with icing sugar and chill until ready to serve.

Variation

As a simple shortcut, pieces of a 'Flake' chocolate bar can be arranged over the log to create a bark effect.